MIDNIGHT GARDEN

COLORING BOOK

Heart & Flower Designs on a Dramatic Black Background

LINDSEY BOYLAN

DOVER PUBLICATIONS, INC.
MINEOLA, NEW YORK

Welcome to the Midnight Garden, where a spectacular array of exotic floral designs and intricate hearts abound! Bursting with coloring possibilities, these curving, swirling, finely detailed images of garden beauties, as well as a profusion of romantic hearts, will charm you, while the intense black background on every page deepens the drama. Just select your media and experiment with the colors of your choice as you embark on this unique collection— plus, the perforated, unbacked pages make displaying your work easy!

Bibliographical Note

*Midnight Garden Coloring Book: Heart & Flower Designs
on a Dramatic Black Background* is a new work,
first published by Dover Publications, Inc., in 2015.

International Standard Book Number

ISBN-13: 978-0-486-80318-0
ISBN-10: 0-486-80318-X

Manufactured in the United States by LSC Communications
80318X05   2019
www.doverpublications.com